Copyright© 2019 By Step

All Rights Reserved

This document is geared towards providing exact and reliable information in regards to the topic and issue covered. The publication is sold with the idea that the publisher is not required to render accounting, officially permitted, or otherwise, qualified services. If advice is necessary, legal or professional, a practiced individual in the profession should be ordered.

From a declaration of principles which was accepted and approved equally by a committee of the American bar association and a committee of publishers and associations.

In no way is it legal to reproduce, duplicate, or transmit any part of this document in either electronic means or in printed format. Recording of this publication is strictly prohibited and any storage of this document is not allowed unless with written permission from the publisher.

The information provided herein is stated to be truthful and consistent, in that any liability, in terms of inattention or otherwise, by any usage or abuse of any policies, processes, or directions contained within is the solitary and utter responsibility of the recipient reader. Under no circumstances will any legal responsibility or blame be held against the publisher for any reparation, damages, or monetary loss due to the information herein, either directly or indirectly.

Table of Contents

Introduction 1

Chapter 1 Understanding the Keto Diet 3

   Keto Diet Desserts: Is It Possible? 4

   The Basic Guidelines 4

   Ingredient Substitutions 5

   Nut and Seed Flour 6

   Oils and Fats 8

   Keto-Friendly Sweeteners 10

   Other Essential Ingredients 11

   Tips When Making Keto-Friendly Desserts 11

Chapter 2 Bread 14

   Pumpkin & Walnut Bread 14

   Easy Keto-Approved Almond Bread 15

   Irish Soda Keto Bread 16

   Aromatic Rosemary Keto Bread 18

   Café Copycat Lemon-Poppy Bread 19

   Keto Approved Focaccia Bread 21

   Appetizing Hot Buns 22

   Ordinary Loaf Bread with Psyllium 23

Chapter 3 Muffins & Cakes 25

   Cheesy Onion Muffins 25

   Blueberry and Lemon Flavor Mug Cake 26

   Cinnamon-Pumpkin Flavored Muffin 27

   Cinnamon-Almond Mug Cake 28

Mouth-Watering Choco Cake in a Mug 29

Green Tea Flavored Mug Cake 30

Vegetarian Choco Lava Cake 31

Caramel Chocolate Chip Muffins 32

Keto Angel Food Cake 33

Strawberry Shortcake in A Mug 34

Coconut Raspberry Cupcake Bites 35

Lemon Blueberry Mug Cake 36

Chapter 4 Ice Cream & Ice Pops 37

Vanilla Keto Ice-Cream 38

Strawberry and Vanilla Ice-Cream Swirl 39

Creamy Chocolate Keto Ice Cream 40

Cookies and Cream Keto Style 41

Coconut Keto Ice Cream 43

Yummy and Creamy Lemon Popsicles 44

Delicious Blackberry Popsicle 45

Mocha Flavored Ice Cream 46

Butter Pecan Ice Cream 47

Pumpkin Pie Flavored Ice Cream 48

Chapter 5 Puddings & Pies 49

Tasty Mocha Flavored Pudding Cake 49

Cinnamon, Chia 'n Almond Milk Pudding 51

Choco 'n Chia Pudding 52

Coconut Milk Pudding 53

Vanilla Jello Keto Way 54

Mud Pie with Delish Frosting 55

Keto Banana Pudding 57

Cherry Pie Bars 58

Chapter 6 Cookies & Bars 59

Limey Coconut Bars 60

Blondie Pecan Bars 61

Lemon 'n Cashew Bars 62

Cream Cheese 'n Coconut Cookies 63

Yummy Cinnamon Pecan Bars 64

Goodness Overload Peanut Butter Cookies 66

Fudgy Almond Bars 67

Low Carb Cookie Dough with Sesame Seeds 68

Coconut Raspberry Bars 69

Fast 'n Easy Cookie in a Mug 70

Chapter 7 Brownies 71

Avocado Based Fudgy Brownies 71

Choco-Coco Bars 73

Brownies with Coco Milk 72

5-Ingredient Keto Brownies 75

Keto Chocolate Banana Brownie 76

Brownie Mug Cake 77

Chapter 8 Fat Bombs 78

Creamy Carrot-Cake Flavored Balls 78

Almond Butter Snack Bombs 79

Cheesy Bacon Fat Balls 80

Cinnamon-Cardamom Fat Balls 81

Cinnamon Vanilla Fat Balls 82

Coconut flakes and Oil Boosters 83

Coco-Ginger Fat Bombs 84

Cinnamon-Coco Fat Bombs 85

Chapter 9 Candy and Confections 87

Delicious Reese Cups 87

Brownie Fudge Keto Style 88

Keto Approved No Nuts Fudge 89

Traditional Doughnuts Keto-Approved 90

Crunchy Toffee Topped Cracker Bites 91

Copycat Keto-Approved Almond Joy 94

Sea Salt 'n Macadamia Choco Barks 95

Keto-Approved Lemon Gummies 96

Keto White Choco Fatty Fudge 97

Keto Approved Mouth-Watering Truffles 98

Keto Dark-Choco Cream Cheese Candy 100

Chapter 10 Custard, Cheesecakes and Mousse 101

Avocado-Based Choco Mousse 101

Orange and Chocolate Mousse 102

Eggnog Keto Custard 99

Sugar Free Chocolate Custard 103

Maple Bacon Custard 104

Keto Lemon Custard 105

No Bake Lemon Cheese-Stard 106

Introduction

The Keto Diet is touted as one of the most revolutionary diet regimens today as it yields many positive results especially among those who have tried it. However, the Keto Diet is not only about eating keto-friendly meals, but it also involves eating the right kinds of desserts. The thing is that while the Keto Diet is all about cutting on carbs, it does not mean that you should deprive yourself of eating desserts. Thankfully, keto-friendly desserts are not as much of a head-scratcher as there are now many keto-friendly desserts that you can make and try. Keto-friendly desserts are one of the many reasons why people are motivated to stay true to their diet. After all, a meal will never be complete without desserts and that this is also true for the Keto Diet. Let this e-book serve as your guide when it comes to learning and making your own keto-friendly desserts.

Chapter 1 Understanding the Keto Diet

Understanding the Keto Diet is the first step to making your very own delicious keto-friendly desserts. As the word implies, "keto" refers to "ketones" that is an alternative source of fuel for the body especially when the glucose is in short supply. When the body consumes too little carbohydrates, the liver produces ketones from fat so that the body can still run despite of its low carb source. While the most conventional situation for the liver to produce ketones is to go through periods of fasting, the Keto Diet does not encourage people to avoid eating for longer periods of time. What this diet does is that it encourages people to consume little to no carbs and increase their intake of healthy fats and protein to push the body to enter ketosis.

By pushing the body to undergo ketosis, it can reap many benefits. One of the benefits of this particular diet is that it can help with the management of weight as well as blood sugar levels. When following the Keto Diet, there are certain foods that can be taken in, particularly healthy fats and protein. However, it is crucial to consume only 50 grams of digestible carbohydrates or lower to maintain ketosis.

Keto Diet Desserts: Is It Possible?

Similar with other diet regimens, there are certain rules that you need to follow in order to be succeed in your endeavors. However, one of the greatest challenges with the Keto Diet is how to make ad prepare keto-friendly desserts. Contrary to what most people think, those who follow the Keto Diet can still enjoy and satisfy their cravings with keto-friendly desserts. When it comes to keto-friendly desserts, there are some things that you need to take note of thus this e-book will serve as your in-depth guide when preparing keto-friendly desserts.

The Basic Guidelines

While it can be cumbersome and challenging for first-timers to know about the extensive guidelines of the Keto Diet, there are some basic rules that should be followed when it comes to preparing keto-friendly meals particularly desserts. Below are the basic guidelines that you need to remember when making your keto desserts.

- **Maintain a net carb consumption of 100 grams daily:** This rule is necessary to avoid kicking your body out of ketosis. This means that you need to avoid altogether sugary foods and all kinds of starchy foods.
- **Avoid processed foods:** Processed foods may be advertised as healthy but most of them contain extraneous ingredients including trans-fat (a bad kind of fat) and artificial sugar.
- **Desserts should be high in fat and moderately high in protein:** Whether you are preparing a full meal or a dessert, it is important to consider the ratio of your macros. Food should be mainly high in healthy fat and moderate in protein as it can be converted into sugar from gluconeogenesis.
- **Make the necessary conversion of ingredients:** whether you are making cookies, pies, or cakes, the Keto Diet requires you to know conversions of conventional ingredients. Unlike conventional cooking, the Keto Diet restricts you from using wheat flour, sugar, and other carb-laden ingredients. The succeeding sections will discuss about important substitutions and conversions so that you can make healthy keto-friendly desserts.

Ingredient Substitutions

Whether you are planning to make your favorite pancakes or cupcakes, turning your favorite conventional dessert recipes into something that is keto-friendly is challenging the fact that most of your favorite desserts are made from sugar and carbs. However, there is still a way to make delicious desserts without kicking your body out from ketosis. All it takes is a little ingenuity and some knowledge in ingredient substitutions. When making keto-friendly desserts, there are few pantry essentials that you need to stock up on. Read on to find out which ingredients you need to have in your kitchen to make keto desserts possible.

Nut and Seed Flour

As grains are discouraged for the Keto Diet, you can make use of many different kinds of flour alternatives. Nut and seed flours can help you recreate your favorite dessert recipes. There are different types of seed flour that you can use including the following:

- **Almond flour:** Almond flour is made from almonds that are ground into flour. Often, almond flour is made by removing the seed coat, which makes it better for baking. A quarter of a cup of almond flour contains 12 grams of fat, 5 grams of protein, and 2 grams of carbohydrates. It contains a lot of fat and does not contain any gluten at all thus making it one of the best flour alternatives when making keto-friendly desserts. When using this flour, you may need to use additional eggs or baking powder in order to give it more volume and structure. Almond flour can be used to make cakes, pancakes, and bread while almond meal can be used to make pie crusts and cookies.

- **Almond meal:** Almond meal should not be mistaken with almond meal that has a coarse texture and is often made together with the seed coat It can also be used to thicken smoothies.
- **Coconut flour:** Coconut flour is rich in healthy fats and it is made from dehydrated coconut meat. Unlike almond flour and other nut flours, it is denser, and it absorbs more liquid. When cooking with coconut flour, use more eggs and extra liquid than usual. In general, recipes that call for coconut flour use less of this ingredient. The correct substitution is to use ¼ or 1/3 cup of coconut flour for every cup of grain-based flour used.
- **Seed flour:** There is a variety of seed flour available in the market that can be used to make delicious keto-friendly desserts. These include those made from pumpkin seeds, sesame seeds, sunflower seeds, and others. Seed flour is perfect for making great keto-friendly pie crusts and bars.
- **Chia and Flax seeds:** Although not really used mainly as keto-friendly flour substitute, both chia and flax seeds are used to bind ingredients together. It can be used as a substitute for eggs especially for people who are following a Vegan Keto Diet. To use chia and flax as binders, use a ratio of 1:2 of chia or flax with water.

Oils and Fats

It is important to take note that oils and fats are not created equally. This means that some kinds of fats used in making desserts are not keto-friendly at all. This is especially true for butter made from grain-fed cattle. It is important to take note that a great keto-friendly dessert should contain healthy fat sources. Saturated fats or those that stay solid at room temperature are great fat sources. Another good fat to use is cold-pressed monosaturated fat. Thus, below are some of the best oils and fats that you can use when making keto-friendly desserts.

- **Coconut oil:** Cold-pressed, organic, and virgin coconut oil is a must-have in making keto-friendly meals including desserts. It is a staple when making chocolate ganache as well as making rich and filling desserts.
- **Butter:** It is crucial to use butter sourced from grass-fed cows because its constitution does not contain too much lactose – a type of sugar or simple carbohydrate obtained from milk. Butter from grass-fed cows infuses a delicious and aromatic appeal to all kinds of food.
- **Ghee:** Ghee is clarified butter that is made by simmering butter in low heat to remove the milk solids and water. This is preferred alternative to grass-fed butter especially among people who suffer from dairy intolerance.
- **Other types of oils:** Aside from those mentioned above, other types of fats that can be used to make keto-friendly desserts include macadamia nut oil, hemp seed oil, and olive oil. However, they are ideal in garnishing meals than cooking.

Keto-Friendly Sweeteners

Perhaps one of the biggest hurdles when making keto-friendly desserts is how to make desserts sweet yet keto-friendly. Fortunately, there are many types of keto-friendly sweeteners that you can use to make your favorite desserts. It is important to take note that when it comes to using keto-friendly sweeteners, using artificial sweeteners should be avoided at all cost. Below are examples of guilt-free sweeteners that you can use. A table for the sweetener conversion is also listed thereafter.

- **Lakanto:** Lakanto is an all-natural sweetener made from the combination of erythritol and monk fruit extract. The sweet taste comes from the natural MoGro sides thus making it low-carb and great for those following the Keto Diet. Aside from benefiting those following the Keto Diet, it can also benefit those who have diabetes. To use this sweetener, use in equal proportions as you would use white sugar.
- **Stevia:** Stevia is a marvelous leaf that is as sweet as sugar. You can grow the herb and use the leaves to make delicious desserts. You can also buy stevia sweeteners from your local health store.

Type of sweetener	Substitution Equivalent Compared to Table Sugar				
	1 Tbsp	**¼ cup**	**1/3 cup**	**½ cup**	**1 cup**
Erythritol	1 Tbsp + 1 tsp	1/3 cup	1/3 cup + 2 Tbsp	2/3 cup	1 1/3 cup
Monk Extract	1/25 tsp	1/6 tsp	¼ tsp	1/3 tsp	2/3 tsp
Lakanto	1 Tbsp	¼ cup	1/3 cup	½ cup	1 cup
Stevia extract	1/8 tsp	½ tsp	2/3 tsp	1 tsp	2 tsp

Other Essential Ingredients

Aside from the basic ingredients already mentioned, it is also important to stock up on other keto-friendly items that will help you make great keto-friendly desserts. Below are other ingredients that you can use to make successful and delicious keto-friendly munchies.

- **Psyllium husk powder:** Aside from being used as a colon cleanser, psyllium husk powder can also give the finished product a crumb-like texture. It can be used to make pies and breads.
- **Xanthan gum:** Conventional thickeners are often starch-based. Instead of using cornstarch or cassava starch to thicken desserts, you can use xanthan gum as a carb-free substitute.

Tips When Making Keto-Friendly Desserts

Making keto-friendly desserts can may require several changes on the procedures. This is to ensure that the ingredients are cooked thoroughly, and that the dessert comes out good. Below are some tips when making keto-friendly desserts.

- When using high fat flour substitute, use less oil but use more binder to provide more structure to the dessert. This is especially true when making breads, muffins, and cakes.
- Add extra raising agent for more volume and structure. Rising agents such as baking powder and baking soda can be helpful in improving the structure of keto-friendly desserts. Omit using yeast because it mainly feeds on the sugar contained in wheat.
- When making batters for pancakes, muffins, or cakes, do not thin out by using too much water. Thinning out the batter would

result to nothing but soggy mess. Low-carb batters need to be thicker than conventional batters.
- When baking keto-friendly cakes and pastries, use a lower temperature (25°F lower) than you would normally bake conventional pastries. Although you will cook for a longer period of time, it will save your desserts from browning too quickly or burning due to high temperature.
- Always allow your keto-friendly desserts (particularly the cooked or baked ones) to sit and cool completely for a few hours to allow them to hold together completely.
- Lastly, store your ingredients properly to avoid them from spoiling. Keto-friendly flours, for instance, have poorer shelf lives compared with wheat flour. Storing them in a cool dark place can improve their shelf lives.

If you are one of the many people who are still skeptical whether you can make delicious keto-friendly desserts, then the next sections in this book will give you details on recipes that you can make and satisfy your cravings for dessert.

Chapter 2 Bread

Pumpkin & Walnut Bread

Serves: 12 slices
Cooking Time: 60 minutes
Ingredients:

- 1 1/2 tsp pumpkin pie spice
- 1 cup pumpkin puree
- 1 pinch sea salt
- 1 tbsp baking powder
- 1/2 cup coconut flour (sifted)
- 1/2 cup erythritol
- 1/3 cup heavy cream
- 1/4 cup chopped walnuts
- 2 cups almond flour
- 3/4 cup melted butter
- 4 large eggs

Directions:

1. Lightly grease a loaf pan and preheat oven to 350OF.
2. In a large mixing bowl, whisk well salt, pumpkin spice, baking powder, sugar free sweetener, coconut flour, and almond flour.
3. In a blender, blend until smooth the eggs, heavy cream, butter, and pumpkin.
4. Pour into bowl of dry ingredients and mix thoroughly.
5. Pour batter in loaf pan and bake for 60 minutes or when poked with a toothpick, it comes out clean.

6. Remove bread from pan.
7. Let it cool. Evenly divide into suggested servings and place in meal prep containers.

Nutrition Information:
Calories per serving: 228; Protein: 5.5g; Fat: 20g; Carbohydrates: 6.5g

Easy Keto-Approved Almond Bread

Serves: 10
Cooking Time: 5 hours
Ingredients:

- 3 large eggs, beaten
- ¼ cup olive oil
- 2 ½ cups almond flour
- 1 ½ cups erythritol
- 1 ½ teaspoon baking powder

Directions:

1. Mix all ingredients in a mixing bowl.
2. Add a pinch of salt and cinnamon if desired.
3. Once properly mixed, pour the batter in a greased pot.
4. Close the lid and make sure that the vent points to "Venting."
5. Press the "Slow Cook" button and adjust the time to 5 hours.

Nutrition Information:
Calories per serving: 68; Carbohydrates: 0.6g; Protein: 0.9g; Fat: 6.9g

Irish Soda Keto Bread

Serves: 8 slices
Cooking Time: 45 minutes

Ingredients:

- ½ cup currants
- ½ tsp nutmeg
- ½ tsp salt
- 1 cup minus 1 tbsp light, canned coconut milk + more for brushing on loaf
- 1 tbsp apple cider vinegar
- 1 tbsp cold butter
- 1 tbsp honey
- 1 tbsp keto mayonnaise
- 1 tsp cinnamon
- 1 tsp gluten free baking powder
- 2 cups almond flour, plus more for kneading
- 2 large lightly beaten eggs
- 2 tsp baking soda

Directions:

1. In medium mixing bowl, sift together nutmeg, cinnamon, baking powder, salt, and flour.
2. With hands, work butter into flour. Add currants
3. Add coconut milk and vinegar and beat well.
4. Add eggs and mayonnaise and beat lightly.
5. Add baking soda and mix.

6. Flour hands with almond flour and knead dough on a floured surface.
7. Shape loaf into a round ball and cut an X on top.
8. Brush dough with coconut milk and let it rise for ten minutes.
9. Preheat oven to 375oF and line a baking sheet with parchment paper and grease lightly with cooking spray.
10. Transfer dough on prepared sheet and brush once more with coconut milk.
11. Pop in the oven and bake for 35 to 45 minutes or until lightly browned on the outside.
12. Remove from oven and pan immediately and let it cool.
13. Serve and enjoy while warm.

Nutrition Information:
Calories per serving: 203; Carbohydrates: 9.9g; Protein: 7g; Fat: 15g

Aromatic Rosemary Keto Bread

Serves: 8 slices
Cooking Time: 45 minutes

Ingredients:

- ½ cup chopped walnuts
- 4 tbsp fresh, chopped rosemary
- 1 1/3 cups lukewarm carbonated water
- 1 tbsp honey
- ½ cup extra virgin olive oil
- 1 tsp apple cider vinegar
- 4 eggs
- 5 tsp instant dry yeast granules
- 1 tsp salt
- 1 tbsp xanthan gum
- ¼ cup buttermilk powder
- 2 cups almond flour
- 2 cups coconut flour, sifted

Directions:

1. In a large mixing bowl, whisk well eggs. Add 1 cup warm water, honey, olive oil, and vinegar.
2. While beating continuously, add the rest of the ingredients except for rosemary and walnuts.
3. Continue beating. If dough is too stiff, add a bit of warm water. Dough should be shaggy and thick.
4. Then add rosemary and walnuts continue kneading until evenly distributed.

5. Cover bowl of dough with a clean towel, place in a warm spot, and let it rise for 30 minutes.
6. Fifteen minutes into rising time, preheat oven to 400oF.
7. Generously grease with olive oil a 2-quart Dutch oven and preheat inside oven without the lid.
8. Once dough is done rising, remove pot from oven, and place dough inside. With a wet spatula, spread top of dough evenly in pot.
9. Brush tops of bread with 2 tbsp of olive oil, cover Dutch oven and bake for 35 to 45 minutes.
10. Once bread is done, remove from oven. And gently remove bread from pot.
11. Allow bread to cool at least ten minutes before slicing.
12. Serve and enjoy.

Nutrition Information:
Calories per serving: 298; Carbohydrates: 7.7g; Protein: 5g; Fat: 27.4g

Café Copycat Lemon-Poppy Bread

Serves: 12 slices
Cooking Time: 50 minutes
Bread Ingredients:

- ½ cup of Sukrin
- ½ teaspoon of Baking Powder
- 2 Lemons, zest only
- 2 tablespoons of Poppy Seeds
- 3 tablespoons of Butter, melted

- 3 tablespoons of Lemon Juice
- 6 Eggs
- 9.5 ounces (3 cups) of Almond Flour

Glaze Ingredients:

- 1 tablespoon of Lemon Juice
- 1/2 cup of Natvia Icing Mix
- 1-2 tablespoons of Water

Directions:

1. Preheat oven to 350oF.
2. In a large mixing bowl, whisk well poppy seeds, sweetener, baking powder, and almond flour.
3. Stir in butter, lemon juice, and lemon zest.
4. Add the eggs and mix until all combined
5. Pour the mixture into your lined 9×5 loaf tin.
6. Bake in the oven for 45-50 minutes. The loaf is cooked when golden brown and springs back when touched.
7. Leave to cool for 20 minutes.
8. For the Glaze: place lemon juice and icing mix in small mixing bowl.
9. Slowly add water until the mixture has a pouring consistency.

Nutrition Information:
Calories per serving: 211; Carbohydrates: 7.5g; Protein: 8.2g; Fat: 16.5g

Keto Approved Focaccia Bread

Serves: 8 slices
Cooking Time: 25 minutes

Ingredients:

- ¼ teaspoon of Xanthan Gum
- ½ teaspoon of Garlic Powder
- 1 ¾ cups of Almond Flour
- 1 teaspoon of Baking Powder
- 16 Kalamata Olives, pitted
- 3 sprigs of Rosemary
- 4 Eggs
- 4 ounces of Cream Cheese, softened
- 4 ounces of Salted Butter, softened

Directions:

1. Preheat oven to 375oF and line an 8x12-in baking pan with parchment paper.
2. Place the cream cheese and butter into a mixing bowl and whip using your hand mixer on high speed, until fluffy.
3. Add the eggs one at a time, beating well every after each addition. Don't worry if the mixture looks curdled, it will come together when the dry ingredients are added.
4. Whisk in garlic powder, xanthan gum, baking powder, and almond flour. Once combined, swap the hand mixer for a spatula and mix well.
5. Scoop the mixture onto your prepared baking tray and smooth out.
6. Top with the rosemary and olives.

7. Place into the oven and bake for 18-25 minutes, the focaccia is cooked when it springs back when touched.
8. Enjoy warm or cool and slice to use for sandwiches.

Nutrition Information:
Calories per serving: 160; Carbohydrates: 2.1g; Protein: 4.4g; Fat: 14.9g

Appetizing Hot Buns

Serves: 8
Cooking Time: 15 minutes
Ingredients:

- 4 eggs, beaten
- 1 cup coconut milk
- 1/3 cup coconut flour
- 3 tablespoons cacao powder
- ¼ cup cacao nibs

Directions:

1. Preheat the air fryer for 5 minutes.
2. Combine all ingredients in a mixing bowl.
3. Form buns using your hands and place in a baking dish that will fit in the air fryer.
4. Bake for 15 minutes for 375oF.
5. Once air fryer turns off, leave the buns in the air fryer until it cools completely.

Nutrition Information:
Calories per serving: 161; Carbohydrates: 4g; Protein: 5.7g; Fat: 13.6g

Ordinary Loaf Bread with Psyllium

Serves: 8
Cooking Time: 20 minutes

Ingredients:

- 1 ½ cups almond flour
- ¼ cup erythritol powder
- 2 tablespoon psyllium husk powder
- ½ cup coconut milk
- 1/3 cup butter, unsalted
- 2 large eggs, beaten
- 1 ½ teaspoon baking powder
- 2 tablespoons poppy seeds
- ¼ teaspoon vanilla extract

Directions:

1. Preheat the air fryer for 5 minutes.
2. In a mixing bowl, combine all ingredients.
3. Use a hand mixer to mix everything.
4. Pour into a small loaf pan that will fit in the air fryer.
5. Bake for 20 minutes at 3750F or until a toothpick inserted in the middle comes out clean.

Nutrition Information:

Calories per serving: 145; Carbohydrates: 3.6; Protein: 2.1g; Fat: 13.6g

Chapter 3 Muffins & Cakes

Cheesy Onion Muffins

Serves: 6
Cooking Time: 20 minutes
Ingredients:

- ¼ cup Colby jack cheese, shredded
- ¼ cup shallots, minced
- ½ tsp salt
- 1 cup almond flour
- 1 egg
- 3 tbsp melted butter
- 3 tbsp sour cream

Directions:

1. Line 6 muffin tins with 6 muffin liners. Set aside and preheat oven to 350oF.
2. In a bowl, stir the dry and wet ingredients alternately. Mix well using a spatula until the consistency of the mixture becomes even.
3. Scoop a spoonful of the batter to the prepared muffin tins.
4. Bake for 20 minutes in oven until golden brown.
5. Let it cool and store in an airtight container.

Nutrition Information:
Calories per serving: 200; Protein: 6.3g; Fat: 17.4g; Carbohydrates: 4.6g

Blueberry and Lemon Flavor Mug Cake

Serves: 5
Cooking Time: 4 minutes

Ingredients:

- ½ cup coconut milk
- ½ cups coconut flour
- ½ teaspoon lemon zest
- 1 teaspoon baking soda
- 4 large eggs

Directions:

1. Combine all ingredients in a mixing bowl.
2. Pour into a mug.
3. Place mug in microwave and cook for 2 minutes.
4. Let it sit for another two minutes to continue cooking, serve and enjoy.

Nutrition Information:
Calories per serving: 259; Carbohydrates: 10.3g; Protein: 7.2g; Fat: 20.9g

Cinnamon-Pumpkin Flavored Muffin

Serves: 10
Cooking Time: 20 minutes

Ingredients:

- 1 1/4 cup flaxseeds (ground)
- 1 cup pure pumpkin puree
- 1 egg
- 1 tbsp cinnamon
- 1 tbsp pumpkin pie spice
- 1/2 tbsp baking powder
- 1/2 tsp apple cider vinegar
- 1/2 tsp salt
- 1/2 tsp vanilla extract
- 1/3 cup erythritol
- 1/4 cup Walden Farm's Maple Syrup
- 2 tbsp coconut oil

Directions:

1. Line ten muffin tins with ten muffin liners and preheat oven to 350oF.
2. In a blender, add all ingredients and blend until smooth and creamy, around 5 minutes.
3. Evenly divide batter into prepared muffin tins.
4. Pop in the oven and bake for 20 minutes or until tops are lightly browned.
5. Let it cool. Evenly divide into suggested servings and place in meal prep containers.

Nutrition Information:
Calories per serving: 117; Protein: 5.0g; Fat: 8.5g; Carbohydrates: 5.0g

Cinnamon-Almond Mug Cake

Serves: 3
Cooking Time: 15 minutes
Ingredients:

- 3 eggs, beaten
- ¼ cup almond powder
- ¼ teaspoon baking powder
- 1 teaspoon cinnamon powder
- Liquid stevia to taste

Directions:

1. Mix all ingredients in a mixing bowl until well-combined.
2. Pour into a greased mug.
3. Place in microwave and cook on high for 2 minutes per mug.
4. Let it sit for 3 minutes after cooking.
5. Serve and enjoy.

Nutrition Information:
Calories per serving: 120; Carbohydrates: 1.7g; Protein: 6.3g; Fat: 9.7g

Mouth-Watering Choco Cake in a Mug

Serves: 1
Cooking Time: 10 minutes

Ingredients:

- 1 egg, beaten
- ¼ cup almond powder
- ¼ teaspoon baking powder
- 1 ½ tablespoon cocoa powder
- Liquid stevia to taste

Directions:

1. Place a steam rack in the Instant Pot and pour a cup of water.
2. Place all ingredients in a mixing bowl. Add a pinch of salt.
3. Mix until well-combined.
4. Pour into a heat-proof mug.
5. Place the mug in microwave.
6. Cook for 2.5 minutes and then let it sit for 3 minutes before enjoying.

Nutrition Information:

Calories per serving: 145; Carbohydrates: 5.8g; Protein: 6.8g; Fat: 10.5g

Green Tea Flavored Mug Cake

Serves: 1
Cooking Time: 12 minutes

Ingredients:

- 1 large egg
- 1 tbsp coconut oil
- 1 tsp baking powder
- 1 pinch sea salt
- 2 tbsp frozen sugar-free white chocolate chips, frozen
- ½ tsp vanilla extract
- ½ tsp matcha powder
- ¼ cup almond flour
- 1/8 tsp xanthan gum
- 5-10 drops liquid stevia
- 1 ½ tbsp powdered erythritol

Directions:

1. Lightly grease the inside of a mug with cooking spray and preheat the oven to 350oF.
2. In a small bowl, whisk well egg, coconut oil, baking powder, salt, vanilla, and liquid stevia.
3. Stir in matcha powder, almond flour, xanthan gum, and erythritol. Mix well.
4. Fold in frozen white Choco chips. Transfer to the prepared mug.
5. Pop in the oven and bake for 12 minutes.
6. Let cool a bit and enjoy.

Nutrition Information:
Calories per serving: 426; Protein: 14.0g; Carbs: 7.0g; Fat: 38.0g

Vegetarian Choco Lava Cake

Serves: 1
Cooking Time: 2 minutes

Ingredients:

- 2 tbsp cocoa powder
- 1 medium egg
- 1 tbsp heavy cream
- 1 pinch salt
- 1-2 tbsp erythritol
- 1/2 tsp vanilla extract
- 1/4 tsp baking powder

Directions:

1. On a small mixing bowl, whisk well cocoa powder and erythritol.
2. In a different bowl, whisk egg until fluffy. Pour into the bowl of cocoa and mix well.
3. Stir in vanilla and heavy cream mix well.
4. Add baking powder and salt. Mix well.
5. Lightly grease a ramekin and pour in batter.
6. Stick in the microwave and cook for a minute on high. Let it rest for a minute.
7. Serve and enjoy.

Nutrition Information:
Calories per serving: 173; Protein: 8.0g; Carbs: 6.0g; Fat: 13.0g

Caramel Chocolate Chip Muffins

Serves: 12
Cooking Time: 25 minutes
Ingredients:

- ¾ cup semi-sweet chocolate chips
- ½ cup caramel dip (Walden Farms SF brand)
- 1 tsp stevia glycerite
- 2 tbsp butter, melted
- 1 cup sour cream
- 2 lightly beaten eggs, large
- ½ tsp xanthan gum
- ½ tsp salt
- ½ tsp baking soda
- 1/8 cup erythritol
- 2 cups almond flour

Directions:
1. In a mixing bowl, mix together erythritol, almond flour, salt, baking soda and xanthan gum. In a separate bowl, beat the eggs, sour cream, butter and stevia.
2. Pour the liquid mixture to the almond flour mixture and fold together until properly blended.
3. Add the chocolate chips last. Mix well.
4. In a prepared muffin tins with liners, fill each muffin cup with the batter about ¾ full.
5. Bake for 20 to 25 minutes inside a 350-degree Fahrenheit preheated oven.
6. Remove from the oven once done and let them cool for an hour before dipping in caramel dip.

Nutrition Information:
Calories per serving: 121; Protein: 2.5g; Carbs: 8.2g; Fat: 8.7g

Keto Angel Food Cake

Serves: 12
Cooking Time: 30 minutes
Ingredients

- 12 egg whites
- 2 teaspoons cream of tartar
- A pinch of salt
- 1 cup powdered erythritol
- 1 teaspoon strawberry extract
- ¼ cup butter, melted

Directions:

1. Preheat the air fryer for 5 minutes.
2. Mix the egg whites and cream of tartar.
3. Use a hand mixer and whisk until white and fluffy.
4. Add the rest of the ingredients except for the butter and whisk for another minute.
5. Pour into a baking dish.
6. Place in the air fryer basket and cook for 30 minutes at 400oF or if a toothpick inserted in the middle comes out clean.
7. Drizzle with melted butter once cooled.

Nutrition Information:
Calories per serving: 65; Carbohydrates: 1.8g; Protein: 3.1g; Fat: 5g

Strawberry Shortcake in A Mug

Serves: 4
Cooking Time: 25 minutes

Ingredients:

- 2/3 cup almond flour
- ½ cup butter
- 3 large eggs, beaten
- 1/3 cup erythritol
- 1 teaspoon vanilla extract
- ¼ teaspoon salt
- ¼ teaspoon liquid stevia
- ½ teaspoon baking powder
- 1 cup strawberries, halved

Directions:

1. Preheat the air fryer for 5 minutes.
2. In a mixing bowl, combine all ingredients except for the strawberries.
3. Use a hand mixer to mix everything.
4. Pour into greased mugs.
5. Top with sliced strawberries
6. Place the mugs in the fryer basket.
7. Bake for 25 minutes at 350oF.
8. Place in the fridge to chill before serving.

Nutrition Information:

Calories per serving: 265; Carbohydrates: 3.7g; Protein:2.5 g; Fat: 26.7g

Coconut Raspberry Cupcake Bites

Serves: 6
Cooking Time: 30 minutes

Ingredients

- 1 cup coconut flour
- 1 cup almond milk, unsweetened
- 7 large eggs, beaten
- ½ cup butter
- 1 tablespoon baking powder
- 3 teaspoons vanilla extract
- ½ teaspoon salt
- ¾ cup erythritol

Directions:

1. Preheat the air fryer for 5 minutes.
2. Mix all ingredients using a hand mixer.
3. Pour into hard cupcake molds.
4. Place in the air fryer basket.
5. Bake for 30 minutes at 350oF or until a toothpick inserted in the middle comes out clean.
6. Bake by batches if possible.
7. Allow to chill before serving.

Nutrition Information:

Calories per serving: 235; Carbohydrates: 7.4g; Protein: 3.8g; Fat: 21.1g

Lemon Blueberry Mug Cake

Serves: 4
Cooking Time: 8 minutes

Ingredients:
- ¼ cup coconut oil
- ¼ cup Swerve sweetener
- ¼ teaspoon lemon extract
- ½ cup blueberries
- ½ cup coconut flour
- 1 teaspoon baking soda
- 1/2cup coconut milk
- 4 large eggs, beaten
- Zest from 1 lemon

Directions:
1. Place a steam rack or trivet in the Instant Pot and pour a cup of water.
2. Combine all ingredients in bowl until well-combined.
3. Pour in heat-proof mugs.
4. Microwave each mug for 2 minutes and let it sit for two minutes before serving.

Nutrition information:
Calories per serving: 274; Carbohydrates: 20.8g; Protein: 4.1g; Fat: 19.4g

Chapter 4 Ice Cream & Ice Pops

Vanilla Keto Ice-Cream

Serves: 6
Cook Time: 0 minutes

Ingredients:

- 1 ¼ cups heavy whipping cream
- 1 tbsp sugar-free vanilla extract 1/2 cup powdered low carb sweetener
- 1/4 tsp cream of tartar
- 4 large eggs

Directions:

1. Mix egg whites, cream, and tartar. Slowly add Erythritol as egg white mixture thickens.
2. In another bowl whisk the cream.
3. Mix the egg yolks in another bowl with vanilla extract/powder.
4. Mix egg whites with the whipped cream. Then add egg yolks.
5. Freeze for at least 2 hours.

Nutrition Information:
Calories per serving: 137: Carbs: 2g; Fats: 13g; Protein: 3g

Strawberry and Vanilla Ice-Cream Swirl

Serves: 6

Cook Time: 0 minutes

Ingredients:
- 1 cup strawberries
- 1 tbsp vodka
- ⅛ tsp xanthan gum
- ½ tsp vanilla extract
- 3 large egg yolks
- ⅓ cup erythritol
- 1 cup heavy cream

Directions:
1. Dissolve erythritol in simmering heavy cream (low flame).
2. Beat egg yolks then add a few tbsp of the hot cream mixture while mixing.
3. When egg mixture is warm slowly add the rest of the cream mix in, do not stop mixing.
4. Add in vanilla extract, vodka, and xanthan gum-- then mix.
5. Freeze for 2 hours.

Nutrition Information:
Calories per serving: 166; Carbs: 2.8 g; Fats: 16.64 g; Protein: 2.64 g

Creamy Chocolate Keto Ice Cream

Serves: 5
Cook Time: 0 minutes

Ingredients:

- Cocoa powder
- 1 ½ tsp vanilla extract
- ⅛ tsp salt
- ⅓ cup erythritol or other sweetener
- 2 cups full fat coconut milk

Directions:

1. Stir milk, salt, vanilla extract, and sweetener together.
2. Freeze for at least an hour.

Nutrition Information:

Calories per serving: 197; Carbs: 4.4 g; Fat: 19.1 g; Protein: 1.8g

Cookies and Cream Keto Style

Serves: 10
Cook Time: 20 minutes

Ingredients for Ice Cream:

- ½ cup almond milk
- ½ cup erythritol
- 1 tbsp vanilla extract
- 2 ½ cups whipping cream

Ingredients for cookies:

- Pinch of salt
- 1 large egg
- 1 ½ tbsp coconut oil
- ½ tsp vanilla extract
- ¼ cup erythritol
- ¼ tsp baking soda
- ¼ cup cocoa powder
- ¾ cup almond flour

Directions:

1. Preheat oven to 300 degrees F.
2. Sift almond flour, baking soda, salt, erythritol, and cocoa powder in a bowl and mix.
3. Mix in coconut oil and vanilla extract until batter becomes fine crumbs.
4. Mix in egg until batter sticks together.
5. Spread batter thinly into cake pan and bake for 20 minutes.
6. Crumble the cookie once done cooking.

7. In a large bowl whip the cream with an electric mixer.
8. Mix in erythritol, almond milk, and vanilla extract.
9. Churn mixture in an ice cream maker, gradually adding in cookie crumbs.
10. Freeze for 2 hours.

Nutrition Information:
Calories per serving: 298; Carbs: 4.7 g; Fats: 29 g; Protein: 4.6 g

Coconut Keto Ice Cream

Serves: 5
Cook Time: 10 minutes

Ingredients:

- 1 tsp vanilla
- 25g shredded coconut
- 4 tbsp powdered sweetener
- 250 ml heavy cream
- 500 ml full fat coconut cream
- 5 egg yolks

Directions:

1. Whisk egg yolks.
2. In low heat simmer sweetener, cream, and coconut cream. Remove from heat once it starts bubbling.
3. Whisk in a spoon of warm cream to egg yolks, gradually adding more until all cream is mixed in.
4. Mix in vanilla. Put back over the heat and thicken to a custard consistency.
5. Mix in shredded coconut.
6. Freeze.

Nutrition Information:
Calories per serving: 417; Carbs: 6.5 g; Fat: 41 g; Protein: 5.5 g

Yummy and Creamy Lemon Popsicles

Serves: 6
Cook Time: 0 minutes

Ingredients:

- 1 ¾ cup heavy whipping cream
- 3 eggs
- 1 cup erythritol
- 1 lemon (juice with zest)

Directions:

1. Separate eggs then beat egg whites. Mix egg yolk and sweetener then add the lemon juice. Mix in egg whites after.
2. Whip heavy cream and then mix in egg mixture.
3. Pour into Popsicle molds.
4. Freeze for 2 hours

Nutrition Information:

Calories per serving: 275; Carbs: 3 g; Fats: 27 g; Protein: 5 g

Delicious Blackberry Popsicle

Serves: 8
Cook Time: 0 minutes
Ingredients:

- 1 large egg yolk
- 1 cup fresh blackberries
- ½ cup powdered erythritol
- 1 ½ cups heavy whipping cream

Directions:

1. Mix all ingredients together using a high-speed blender for 2 to 3 minutes.
2. Pour into popsicle molds.
3. Freeze for at least 2 hours or use ice cream maker.

Nutrition Information:
Calories per serving: 196: Carbs: 4g; Fats: 20g; Protein: 0g

Mocha Flavored Ice Cream

Serves: 8
Cook time: 0 minutes
Ingredients:

- 1 tsp vanilla extract
- 2 tbsp cocoa powder
- 2 tbsp espresso powder
- 1 egg yolk
- ½ cup erythritol
- 2 cups heavy whipping cream

Directions:

1. Mix all ingredients together until smooth.
2. Freeze until desired consistency is achieved.

Nutrition Information:
Calories per serving: 52; Carbs: 4g; Fats: 4g; Protein: 0g

Butter Pecan Ice Cream

Serves: 8
Cook Time: 10 minutes
Ingredients:

- 1 tsp vanilla extract
- 6 tbsp butter
- ¼ cup erythritol
- ½ cup chopped pecans
- 1 ½ cup heavy whipping cream

Directions:

1. Melt butter in low heat then bring to rolling boil when putting in chopped pecans for 3-5 minutes. Wait until butter browns. Then let pecans cool.
2. Mix all ingredients together including pecans.
3. Freeze or use ice cream maker.

Nutrition Information:
Calories per serving: 43; Carbs: 3g; Fats: 3g; Protein: 1g

Pumpkin Pie Flavored Ice Cream

Serves: 8
Cook Time: 0 minutes

Ingredients:

- 3 tsp pumpkin pie spice
- 2 egg yolks
- ½ cup erythritol
- ¼ cup pumpkin puree
- 2 cups heavy whipping cream

Directions:

1. Mix all ingredients together.
2. Freeze or use ice cream maker.

Nutrition Information:
Calories per serving: 52; Carbs: 4g; Fats: 4g; Protein: 0g

Chapter 5 Puddings & Pies

Tasty Mocha Flavored Pudding Cake

Serves: 9
Cooking Time: 20 minutes
Ingredients:

- ½ cup heavy cream
- ¾ cup butter
- 1 teaspoon vanilla extract
- 1/3 cup almond flour
- 1/8 teaspoon salt

- 2 tablespoons instant coffee crystals
- 2/3 cup granulated sweetener
- 2-ounces unsweetened chocolate
- 4 tablespoons unsweetened cocoa powder
- 5 large eggs
- Coconut oil spray

Directions:

1. Lightly grease a 9x9-inch square pan and preheat oven to 350oF.
2. Place butter in a microwave safe bowl and melt. Once melted, stir in chocolate and mix well. If needed, heat again in 10-second intervals to melt the chocolate.
3. In a mixing bowl, whisk well the eggs until pale. Slowly add the sweetener while beating continuously.
4. Beat in heavy cream, coffee crystals, and vanilla.
5. Beat in melted butter and chocolate mixture.
6. Stir in cocoa powder, almond flour, and salt. Mix thoroughly.
7. Pour batter into prepared pan and bake in the oven for 20 minutes.
8. Let it cool, evenly divide into suggested servings, and store in meal prep ready container.

Nutrition Information:
Calories per serving: 265.7; Protein: 2.4g; Fat: 20.8g; Carbohydrates: 18.6g

Cinnamon, Chia 'n Almond Milk Pudding

Serves: 2
Cooking Time: 0 minutes

Ingredients:

- 1/2 teaspoon cinnamon powder
- 1/3 cup (78 ml) of coconut or almond milk
- 1/8 teaspoon vanilla extract
- 2 Tablespoons chia seeds
- 2 teaspoons unsweetened cacao powder
- Stevia to taste

Directions:

1. In a small bowl, mix well milk, vanilla, cinnamon, chia and cacao powder.
2. Refrigerate for 4 hours.
3. Evenly divide into suggested servings and store in meal prep ready container.

Nutrition Information:
Calories per serving: 77; Protein: 3g; Fat: 5g; Carbohydrates: 6g

Choco 'n Chia Pudding

Serves: 4
Cooking Time: 3 hours
Ingredients:

- ¼ cup chia seeds
- ½ teaspoon liquid stevia
- 1 cup coconut milk, freshly squeezed
- 2 tablespoons cacao powder
- A pinch of salt

Directions:

1. Pour everything in a slow cooker.
2. Give a good stir.
3. Cover and press low settings and adjust the time to 3 hours.

Nutrition Information:
Calories per serving: 346; Carbohydrates: 21.2g; Protein: 8.4g; Fat: 27.5g

Coconut Milk Pudding

Serves: 2
Cooking Time: 10 minutes

Ingredients:

- ½ teaspoon vanilla extract
- 1 ½ cup coconut milk
- 1 tablespoon gelatin, unsweetened
- 2 teaspoons erythritol
- 3 egg yolks, beaten

Directions:

1. Place the coconut milk in the Instant Pot.
2. Close the lid and make sure that the vent points to "Sealing."
3. Press the "Manual" button and adjust the time to 5 minutes.
4. Do quick pressure release.
5. Once the lid is open, press the "Sauté" button.
6. Allow to simmer and whisk gradually the egg yolks. Keep stirring vigorously.
7. Add the gelatin, sweetener, and vanilla extract.
8. Stir for 3 minutes.
9. Place in ramekins and allow to cool for an hour.

Nutrition Information:

Calories per serving: 529; Carbohydrates: 12.2g; Protein: 8.3g; Fat: 49.7g

Vanilla Jello Keto Way

Serves: 6
Cooking Time: 6 minutes

Ingredients:

- 1 cup boiling water
- 1 cup heavy cream
- 1 teaspoon vanilla extract
- 2 tablespoons gelatin powder, unsweetened
- 3 tablespoons erythritol

Directions:

1. Place the boiling water in the Instant Pot.
2. Press the "Sauté" button on the Instant Pot and allow the water to simmer.
3. Add the gelatin powder and allow to dissolve.
4. Stir in the rest of the ingredients.
5. Pour the mixture into jello molds.
6. Place in the fridge to set for 2 hours.

Nutrition Information:
Calories per serving: 105; Carbohydrates: 5.2g; Protein: 3.3; Fat: 7.9g

Mud Pie with Delish Frosting

Serves: 10
Cooking Time: 40 minutes

Ingredients:

- 1 ½ tsp baking soda
- 1 cup butter (melted)
- 1 cup erythritol
- 1/2 cup cocoa powder (sifted)
- 1/2 cup heavy cream
- 1/2 tsp salt
- 1/4 cup almond milk
- 2 cups almond flour
- 2 tbsp coconut flour
- 2 tsp vanilla extract
- 3 large eggs

Frosting Ingredients:

2 tbsp almond milk
1 1/2 tbsp cocoa powder
1/2 cup powdered erythritol
1/4 cup butter

Directions:

1. Lightly grease a 9x9-inch baking dish with cooking spray and preheat the oven to 350oF.
2. In a mixing bowl, whisk well melted butter and eggs. Stir in heavy cream, baking soda, salt, almond milk, and vanilla extract, Mix thoroughly.

3. Add erythritol, cocoa powder, almond flour, and coconut flour. Mix well.
4. Pour into the prepared dish and pop in the oven. Bake for 40 minutes and cool completely.
5. Meanwhile, make the frosting by melting butter in sauce pan. Turn off the fire and whisk in cocoa powder. Mix well.
6. Add almond milk and powdered erythritol and mix thoroughly until glossy and smooth.
7. Pour frosting on top of cake and refrigerate for at least an hour.
8. Slice into suggested servings and enjoy.

Nutrition Information:
Calories per serving: 412; Protein: 7.0g; Carbs: 6.0g; Fat: 40.0g

Keto Banana Pudding

Serves: 1
Cooking Time: 5 minutes
Ingredients:

- 1 large egg yolk
- 3 tbsp powdered erythritol
- 1/2 cup heavy cream
- 1/2 tsp banana extract
- 1/2 tsp xanthan gum

Directions:

1. Place a large saucepan with 1-inch of water on medium-high the fire. Place a small pot inside the saucepan.
2. Add powdered erythritol, egg yolk, and heavy cream in small pot. Whisk well to mix and continue whisking until thickened.
3. Stir in xanthan gum and continue whisking to mix and thicken more.
4. Add salt and banana extract. Mix well.
5. Transfer to a small bowl and cover top completely with cling wrap.
6. Refrigerate for 4 hours and enjoy.

Nutrition Information:
Calories per serving: 439; Protein: 3.0g; Carbs: 5.5g; Fat: 45.0g

Cherry Pie Bars

Serves: 12
Cooking Time: 35 minutes

Ingredients:

- ½ cup butter, softened
- 1 cup erythritol
- ½ teaspoon salt
- 2 eggs
- ½ teaspoon vanilla
- 1 ½ cups almond flour
- 1 cup fresh cherries, pitted
- ¼ cup water
- 1 tablespoon xanthan gum

Directions:

1. In a mixing bowl, combine the first 6 ingredients until you form a dough.
2. Press the dough in a baking dish that will fit in the air fryer.
3. Place in the air fryer and bake for 10 minutes at 375ºF.
4. Meanwhile, mix the cherries, water, and xanthan gum in a bowl.
5. Take the dough out and pour over the cherry mixture.
6. Return to the air fryer and cook for 25 minutes more at 375ºF.

Nutrition Information:
Calories per serving: 99; Carbohydrates: 2.1g; Protein: 1.8g; Fat: 9.3g

Chapter 6 Cookies & Bars

Limey Coconut Bars

Serves: 16
Cooking Time: 25 minutes
Ingredients:

- 1 1/4 cup Swerve sweetener divided
- 1 tablespoon lime zest
- 1/2 cup lime juice
- 1/2 teaspoon coconut stevia
- 1/4 cup coconut oil room temperature
- 1/4 cup sesame flour or almond flour
- 1/4 cup unsweetened coconut flakes
- 1/4 teaspoon sea salt
- 3/4 cup coconut flour
- 4 eggs

Directions:

1. Lightly grease an 8x8-inch baking pan and preheat oven to 350oF.
2. In a blender, pulse coconut oil, salt, ¼ cup swerve sweetener, sesame flour, and coconut flour. Press on bottom of prepared pan. Bake until lightly browned, around 10 minutes.
3. Meanwhile, in a bowl, whisk well coconut stevia, 1 cup Swerve, lime zest, lime juice, add eggs. Pour this on baked crust.
4. Evenly spread coconut flakes on top and pop in the oven until the center is set, around 13 to 15 minutes.

5. Let it cool, evenly divide into suggested servings, and store in meal prep ready container.

Nutrition Information:
Calories per serving: 102; Protein: 3.5g; Fat: 7.2g; Carbohydrates: 5.7g

Blondie Pecan Bars

Serves: 16
Cooking Time: 30 minutes
Ingredients:

- ¼ cup heavy whipping cream
- ¼ teaspoon salt
- ¾ cup stevia
- 1 ½ cups all-purpose flour
- 1 cup pecans, chopped
- 1 tablespoon cinnamon
- 1 teaspoon baking powder
- 2 teaspoon vanilla extract
- 3 large eggs
- 6 tablespoons unsalted butter, melted

Directions:

1. Preheat oven to 350oF and lightly grease a medium rectangular baking pan.
2. In a large mixing bowl, whisk well eggs until fluffy.
3. Stir in whipping cream, salt, stevia, baking powder, butter, and vanilla. Mix thoroughly.

4. Add remaining ingredients and mix thoroughly.
5. Pour in prepared pan and pop in the oven.
6. Bake for 30 minutes or until when toothpick is inserted in the middle comes out clean.
7. Let it cool, evenly divide into suggested servings, and store in meal prep ready container.

Nutrition Information:
Calories per serving: 211; Protein: 4.4g; Fat: 20.6g; Carbohydrates: 1.9g

Lemon 'n Cashew Bars

Serves: 12
Cooking Time: 25 minutes
Ingredients:

- ¼ cup cashew
- ¼ cup fresh lemon juice, freshly squeezed
- ¾ cup coconut milk
- ¾ cup erythritol
- 1 cup desiccated coconut
- 1 teaspoon baking powder
- 2 eggs, beaten
- 2 tablespoons coconut oil
- A dash of salt

Directions:
1. Preheat oven to 350oF and lightly grease an 8x8-inch square pan.
2. Combine thoroughly all ingredients in a mixing bowl.

3. Pour batter in prepared pan and bake for 20-25 minutes.
4. Let it cool, evenly divide into suggested servings, and store in meal prep ready container.

Nutrition Information:
Calories per serving: 118; Protein: 2.6g; Fat: 10.2g; Carbohydrates: 3.9g

Cream Cheese 'n Coconut Cookies

Serves: 15
Cooking Time: 17 minutes
Ingredients:

- 1 Egg
- 1 teaspoon Vanilla extract
- 1/2 cup Butter softened
- 1/2 cup Coconut Flour
- 1/2 cup Erythritol or other sugar substitute
- 1/2 teaspoon baking powder
- 1/4 teaspoon salt
- 3 tablespoons Cream cheese, softened

Directions:

1. In a mixing bowl, whisk well erythritol, cream cheese, and butter.
2. Add egg and vanilla. Beat until thoroughly combined.
3. Mix in salt, baking powder, and coconut flour.
4. On an 11x13-inch piece of wax paper, place the batter. Mold into a log shape and then twist the ends to secure. Refrigerate for an hour and then slice into 1-cm circles.

5. When ready, preheat oven to 350oF and line a baking sheet with foil. Place cookies at least 1/2-inch apart.
6. Pop in the oven and bake until golden brown, around 17 minutes.
7. Let it cool, evenly divide into suggested servings, and store in meal prep ready container.

Nutrition Information:
Calories per serving: 88; Protein: 1g; Fat: 8g; Carbohydrates: 3g

Yummy Cinnamon Pecan Bars

Serves: 16
Cooking Time: 3 hours
Ingredients:

- ¼ cup heavy whipping cream
- ¼ teaspoon salt
- 1 ½ cups almond flour
- 1 cup pecans, chopped
- 1 cup stevia sweetener
- 1 tablespoon cinnamon
- 1 teaspoon baking powder
- 2 tablespoons unsalted butter
- 2 teaspoons vanilla extract
- 3 large eggs
- 6 tablespoons unsalted butter, melted

Directions:

1. Grease the crockpot with butter.

2. In a bowl, combine the stevia sweetener and melted butter. Add in the eggs and vanilla extract.
3. Use a hand mixer to combine the ingredients.
4. In another bowl, combine the almond flour, salt, baking powder, and cinnamon.
5. Mix the wet ingredients to the dry ingredients until combined.
6. Pour the dough in the crockpot and press to form a dense bar.
7. Cook on low for 3 hours.
8. Meanwhile, mix the butter, whipping cream and pecans in a saucepan. Allow to boil and reduce slightly.
9. Once the bars are cooked, pour over the pecan sauce.
10. Let it cool, evenly divide into suggested servings, and store in meal prep ready container.

Nutrition Information:
Calories per serving: 211; Protein: 4.4g; Fat: 20.6g; Carbohydrates: 1.9g

Goodness Overload Peanut Butter Cookies

Serves: 24
Cooking Time: 15 minutes
Ingredients:

- ¼ tsp salt
- 1 cup unsweetened peanut butter
- 1 tsp baking soda
- 1 tsp stevia powder
- 1/8 tsp xanthan gum
- 2 cups almond flour
- 2 large eggs
- 2 tbsp butter
- 2 tsp pure vanilla extract
- 4 ounces softened cream cheese
- 5 drops liquid Splenda

Directions:

1. Line a cookie sheet with a non-stick liner. Set aside.
2. In a bowl, mix xanthan gum, flour, salt and baking soda. Set aside.
3. On a mixing bowl, combine the butter, cream cheese and peanut butter.
4. Mix on high speed until it forms a smooth consistency. Add the sweetener. Add the eggs and vanilla gradually while mixing until it forms a smooth consistency.
5. Add the almond flour mixture slowly and mix until well combined.
6. The dough is ready once it starts to stick together into a ball.

7. Scoop the dough using a 1 tablespoon cookie scoop and drop each cookie on the prepared cookie sheet. You will make around 24 cookies
8. Press the cookie with a fork and bake for 10 to 12 minutes at 350OF.
9. Let it cool and place in an airtight container.

Nutrition Information:
Calories per serving: 95; Protein: 3.7g; Fat: 6.8g; Carbohydrates: 4.7g

Fudgy Almond Bars

Serves: 8
Cooking Time: 10 minutes
Ingredients:

- 1 cup almond flour
- 1 ounce 80% dark chocolate or sugar-free chocolate chips
- 1/2 cup almond butter
- 1/2 cup unsalted butter (melted and divided)
- 1/2 teaspoon ground cinnamon
- 1/2 teaspoon vanilla extract
- 1/4 cup heavy cream
- 1/8 teaspoon xanthan gum
- 6 tablespoons powdered erythritol (divided)

Directions:

1. Line a 9x10-inch baking dish and preheat the oven to 400oF.
2. In a medium mixing bowl, whisk well cinnamon, 2 tbsp powdered erythritol, ¼ cup melted butter, and almond flour.

3. Evenly spread mixture on bottom of the prepared pan and pop in the oven. Bake until golden brown, about 10 minutes. Once done, remove from the oven and cool completely.
4. In another mixing bowl, beat well 4 tbsp powdered erythritol, remaining butter, almond butter, and heavy cream. Stir in xanthan gum and vanilla. Mix well.
5. Evenly spread mixture on top of cooled crust.
6. Sprinkle Choco chips and refrigerate overnight.
7. Evenly slice into 8 bars and enjoy.

Nutrition Information:
Calories per serving: 235; Protein: 4.5g; Carbs: 4.0g; fat: 22.3g

Low Carb Cookie Dough with Sesame Seeds

Serves: 12
Cooking Time: 20 minutes
Ingredients:

- ¼ cup butter
- ¼ teaspoon xanthan gum
- ½ teaspoon coffee espresso powder
- ½ teaspoon stevia powder
- ¾ cup almond flour
- 1 egg
- 1 teaspoon vanilla
- 1/3 cup sesame seeds
- 2 tablespoons cocoa powder

- 2 tablespoons cream cheese, softened

Instructions:

1. Preheat the air fryer for 5 minutes.
2. Combine all ingredients in a mixing bowl.
3. Press into a baking dish that will fit in the air fryer.
4. Place in the air fryer basket and cook for 20 minutes at 400oF or if a toothpick inserted in the middle comes out clean.

Nutrition Information:
Calories per serving: 88; Carbohydrates: 1.3g; Protein: 1.9g; Fat: 8.3g

Coconut Raspberry Bars

Serves: 12
Cooking Time: 20 minutes
Ingredients:

- 1 cup coconut milk
- ¼ cup coconut oil
- 3 cups desiccated coconut
- 1/3 cup erythritol powder
- 1 teaspoon vanilla bean
- 1 cup raspberries, pulsed

Directions:

1. Preheat the air fryer for 5 minutes.
2. Combine all ingredients in a mixing bowl.

3. Pour into a greased baking dish.
4. Bake in the air fryer for 20 minutes at 375 0F.

Nutrition Information:
Calories per serving: 132; Carbohydrates: 9.7g; Protein: 1.5g; Fat: 9.7g

Fast 'n Easy Cookie in a Mug

Serves: 1
Cooking Time: 10 minutes
Ingredients:

- 1 tablespoon butter
- 3 tablespoons almond flour
- 1 tablespoon erythritol
- A dash of cinnamon
- 1 egg yolk
- 1/8 teaspoon vanilla extract
- A pinch of salt

Directions:

1. Preheat the air fryer for 5 minutes.
2. Combine all ingredients in a mixing bowl.
3. Place in greased mug.
4. Bake in the air fryer for 10 minutes at 375 0F.

Nutrition Information:
Calories per serving: 180; Carbohydrates: 1.4g; Protein: 3.5g; Fat: 17.8g

Chapter 7 Brownies

Avocado Based Fudgy Brownies

Serves: 12
Cooking Time: 35 minutes
Ingredients:

- 1 tsp baking powder
- 1 tsp stevia powder
- 1/2 tsp vanilla
- 1/4 cup erythritol
- 1/4 tsp baking soda
- 1/4 tsp salt
- 100 g lily's dark chocolate melted
- 2 eggs
- 250 g avocado about 2
- 3 tbsp refined coconut oil
- 4 tbsp cocoa powder
- 90 g blanched almond flour

Directions:

1. Lightly grease a 9x9-inch baking pan and preheat oven to 350oF.
2. In a blender or food processor, process the avocados until smooth.
3. Add eggs, coconut oil, salt, vanilla, baking soda, baking powder, erythritol, and melted chocolate. Process again until smooth.
4. Add cocoa powder and almond flour. Process until smooth.
5. Transfer to prepared pan.

6. Bake for 35 minutes.
7. Let it cool, evenly divide into suggested servings, and store in meal prep ready container.

Nutrition Information:
Calories per serving: 180; Protein: 3.8g; Fat: 14.3g; Carbohydrates: 9.0g

Brownies with Coco Milk

Serves: 10
Cooking Time: 6 hours
Ingredients:

- ¾ cup coconut milk
- 1 teaspoon erythritol
- 2 tablespoons butter, melted
- 4 egg yolks, beaten
- 5 tablespoons cacao powder

Directions:

1. In a bowl, mix well all ingredients.
2. Lightly grease your slow cooker with cooking spray and pour in batter.
3. Cover and cook on low for six hours.
4. Let it cool, evenly divide into suggested servings, and store in meal prep ready container.

Nutrition Information:
Calories per serving: 86; Protein: 1.5g; Fat: 8.4g; Carbohydrates: 1.2g

Choco-Coco Bars

Serves: 12
Cooking Time: 0 minutes

Ingredients:

- 1 tablespoon coconut oil
- 1/3 c Virgin Coconut Oil, melted
- 2 cups shredded unsweetened coconut
- 2 droppers Liquid Stevia
- 2 droppers of Liquid Stevia (or enough sweetener to equal 1/4 cup)
- 3 squares Baker's Unsweetened Chocolate (3 ounces chocolate)

Directions:

1. Lightly grease an 8x8-inch silicone pan.
2. In a food processor, process shredded unsweetened coconut, coconut oil, and Stevia until it forms a dough. Transfer to prepared pan and press on bottom to form a dough. Place in the freezer to set.
3. Meanwhile, in a microwave safe Pyrex cup, place chocolate, coconut oil, and Stevia. Heat for 10-second intervals and mix well. Do not overheat, just until you have mixed the mixture thoroughly. Pour over dough.
4. Return to freezer until set.
5. Evenly divide into suggested servings, and store in meal prep ready container.

Nutrition Information:

Calories per serving: 222; Protein: 2g; Fat: 22g; Carbohydrates: 4g

5-Ingredient Keto Brownies

Serves: 9
Cooking Time: 5 hours
Ingredients:

- ¼ cup almond flour
- ½ cup coconut oil
- 1/3 cup dark chocolate chips
- 2 teaspoons erythritol
- 5 eggs, beaten

Directions:

1. Place all ingredients in a mixing bowl.
2. Season with a pinch of salt.
3. Make sure that everything is well-combined.
4. Pour into the greased slow cooker.
5. Cover and press low and adjust the time to 5 hours.

Nutrition Information:

Calories per serving: 222; Carbohydrates: 3.4g; Protein: 5.4g; Fat: 20.7g

Keto Chocolate Banana Brownie

Serves: 12
Cooking Time: 30 minutes

Ingredients:

- 2 cups almond flour
- 2 teaspoons baking powder
- ½ teaspoon baking powder
- ½ teaspoon baking soda
- ½ teaspoon salt
- 1 over-ripe banana
- 3 large eggs
- ½ teaspoon stevia powder
- ¼ cup coconut oil
- 1 tablespoon vinegar
- 1/3 cup almond flour
- 1/3 cup cocoa powder

Directions:

1. Preheat the air fryer for 5 minutes.
2. Combine all ingredients in a food processor and pulse until well-combined.
3. Pour into a baking dish that will fit in the air fryer.
4. Place in the air fryer basket and cook for 30 minutes at 350oF or if a toothpick inserted in the middle comes out clean.

Nutrition Information:
Calories per serving: 75; Carbohydrates: 2.1g; Protein: 1.7g; Fat: 6.6g

Brownie Mug Cake

Serves: 1
Cooking Time: 10 minutes

Ingredients:

- 1 egg, beaten
- ¼ cup almond flour
- ¼ teaspoon baking powder
- ¼ teaspoon vanilla extract
- 1 ½ tablespoons cacao powder
- 1 teaspoon cinnamon powder
- 2 tablespoons stevia powder
- A pinch of salt

Directions:

1. Combine all ingredients in a bowl until well-combined.
2. Transfer in a heat-proof mug.
3. Place the mug in microwave.
4. Cook for 2 minutes. Let it sit for another 2 minutes to continue cooking.
5. Serve and enjoy.

Nutrition Information:
Calories per serving: 159; Carbohydrates: 4.1g; Protein: 9.1g; Fat: 11.8g

Chapter 8 Fat Bombs

Creamy Carrot-Cake Flavored Balls

Serves: 16
Cooking Time: 0 minutes
Ingredients:

- 1 (8-oz) block cream cheese, softened
- 1 cup grated carrots
- 1 cup shredded unsweetened coconut
- 1 teaspoon cinnamon
- 1 teaspoon stevia
- 1/2 cup chopped pecans
- 1/2 teaspoon pure vanilla extract
- 1/4 teaspoon ground nutmeg
- 3/4 cup coconut flour

Directions:

1. In a medium mixing bowl, beat cream cheese, stevia, cinnamon, vanilla, nutmeg, and coconut flour.
2. Fold in pecans and carrots.
3. Evenly divide into 16 portions and roll into balls. Roll balls until covered with shredded coconut.
4. Store in meal prep ready container.

Nutrition Information:
Calories per serving: 106; Protein: 1.7g; Fat: 8.6g; Carbohydrates: 5.5g

Almond Butter Snack Bombs

Serves: 30
Cooking Time: 5 minutes

Ingredients:

- 1 cup almond butter
- 1 cup coconut oil, at room temperature
- 1/16 tsp pink Himalayan salt
- 1/2 cup unsweetened cocoa powder
- 1/3 cup coconut flour
- 1/4 tsp powdered stevia

Directions:

1. In a small pot on medium fire, melt and mix coconut oil and almond butter.
2. Once thoroughly combined, mix in the rest of the ingredients.
3. You can choose to roll the bombs in balls or pour them in a silicon mold.
4. If you want to pour it in molds, do it now and then freeze for 90 minutes approximately.
5. If planning to roll, pour mixture in a bowl and let it freeze for 90 minutes. Afterwards, remove from freezer and roll into 30 balls.
6. Store in meal prep ready container.

Nutrition Information:

Calories per serving: 127; Protein: 2.0g; Fat: 12.1g; Carbohydrates: 2.5g

Cheesy Bacon Fat Balls

Serves: 10
Cooking Time: 8 minutes
Ingredients:

- ½ tsp chili flakes (optional)
- ½ tsp pepper (optional)
- 5 1⁄3-oz bacon
- 5 1⁄3-oz cheddar cheese
- 5 1⁄3-oz cream cheese

Directions:

1. Pan fry bacon until crisped, around 8 minutes.
2. Meanwhile, in a food processor, process remaining ingredients. Then transfer to a bowl and refrigerate. When ready to handle, form into 20 equal balls.
3. Once bacon is cooked, crumble bacon and spread on a plate.
4. Roll the balls on the crumbled bacon to coat.
5. Store in airtight meal prep containers.

Nutrition Information:
Calories per serving: 227; Protein: 6.4g; Fat: 21.6g; Carbohydrates: 1.6g

Cinnamon-Cardamom Fat Balls

Serves: 10
Cooking Time: 3 minutes

Ingredients:

- ¼ tsp ground cardamom (green)
- ¼ tsp ground cinnamon
- ½ cup unsweetened shredded coconut
- ½ tsp vanilla extract
- 3-oz unsalted butter, room temperature

Directions:

1. Place a nonstick pan on medium fire and toast coconut until lightly browned.
2. In a bowl, mix all ingredients.
3. Evenly roll into 10 equal balls.
4. Let it cool in the fridge.
5. Store in an airtight meal prep container.

Nutrition Information:
Calories per serving: 93; Protein: 0.4g; Fat: 10g; Carbohydrates: 0.4g

Cinnamon Vanilla Fat Balls

Serves: 8
Cooking Time: 5 minutes

Ingredients

- 1 cup shredded coconut
- ½ cup coconut oil
- 2 scoops collagen powder
- 2 tablespoons stevia powder
- 1 teaspoon vanilla extract
- 3 tablespoons water
- ½ teaspoon ground cinnamon
- A dash of salt
- 1/3 cup ghee

Directions:

1. Place all ingredients in a mixing bowl until all ingredients are well-combined.
2. Form small balls with the mixture and place in container.
3. Freeze the balls until ready to consume.

Nutrition Information:

Calories per serving: 198; Carbohydrates: 1.3g; Protein: 0.3g; Fat: 21.3g

Coconut flakes and Oil Boosters

Serves: 4
Cooking Time: 10 minutes
Ingredients:

- ½ cup coconut flakes, unsweetened
- 1 cup coconut oil
- 1 teaspoon vanilla extract
- 20 drops liquid stevia
- 3 eggs, beaten

Directions:

1. Combine all ingredients in a mixing bowl.
2. Form balls using your hands.
3. Place on a baking sheet and cook in a 350oF preheated oven for 10 minutes or until golden brown.

Nutrition Information:
Calories per serving: 636; Carbohydrates: 6.4g; Protein: 7.1g; Fat: 64.7g

Coco-Ginger Fat Bombs

Serves: 10
Cooking Time: 10 minutes

Ingredients:

- 1 cup coconut oil
- 1 cup shredded coconut
- 1 teaspoon erythritol
- 1 teaspoon ginger powder

Directions:

1. Add all ingredients and pour ¼ cup water in a saucepan on medium low fire.
2. Stir constantly for 10 minutes.
3. Turn off and scoop small balls from the mixture.
4. Allow to set in the fridge for 1 hour.

Nutrition Information:

Calories per serving: 126; Carbohydrates: 2.2g; Protein: 0.5g; Fat: 12.8g

Cinnamon-Coco Fat Bombs

Serves: 14
Cooking Time: 10 minutes

Ingredients:

- ½ teaspoon cinnamon
- 1 cup coconut butter
- 1 cup coconut milk
- 1 cup coconut shreds
- 1 teaspoon vanilla extract

Directions:

1. Add all ingredients and pour ¼ cup water in a saucepan on medium low fire.
2. Stir constantly for 10 minutes.
3. Turn off and scoop small balls from the mixture.
4. Allow to set in the fridge for 1 hour.

Nutrition Information:

Calories per serving: 196; Carbohydrates: 4.2g; Protein: 0.7g; Fat: 19.6g

Chapter 9 Candy and Confections

Delicious Reese Cups

Serves: 12
Cooking Time: 1 minute
Ingredients:

- ½ cup unsweetened shredded coconut
- 1 cup almond butter
- 1 cup dark chocolate chips
- 1 tablespoon coconut oil
- 1 tablespoon Stevia

Directions:

1. Line 12 muffin tins with 12 muffin liners.
2. Place the almond butter, honey and oil in a glass bowl and microwave for 30 seconds or until melted. Divide the mixture into 12 muffin tins. Let it cool for 30 minutes in the fridge.
3. Add the shredded coconuts and mix until evenly distributed.
4. Pour the remaining melted chocolate on top of the coconuts. Freeze for an hour.
5. Carefully remove the chocolates from the muffin tins to create perfect Reese cups.
6. Store in airtight meal prep containers.

Nutrition Information:
Calories per serving: 229; Protein: 5.0g; Fat: 17.1g; Carbohydrates: 13.7g

Brownie Fudge Keto Style

Serves: 10
Cooking Time: 6 hours

Ingredients:

- ¾ cup coconut milk
- 1 teaspoon erythritol
- 2 tablespoons butter, melted
- 4 egg yolks, beaten
- 5 tablespoons cacao powder

Directions:

1. Place all ingredients in the Instant Pot and mix until well combined.
2. Pour the batter into the greased inner pot.
3. Close the lid and make sure that the vent points to "Venting."
4. Press the "Slow Cook" button and adjust the time to 6 hours.

Nutrition Information:
Calories per serving: 86; Carbohydrates: 1.2g; Protein: 1.5g; Fat: 8.4g

Keto Approved No Nuts Fudge

Serves: 15
Cooking Time: 4 hours

Ingredients:

- ¼ cup cocoa powder
- ½ teaspoon baking powder
- 1 stick of butter, melted
- 4 tablespoons erythritol
- 6 eggs, beaten

Directions:

1. Mix all ingredients in a slow cooker.
2. Add a pinch of salt.
3. Mix until well combined.
4. Cover pot.
5. Press the low settings and adjust the time to 4 hours.

Nutrition Information:

Calories per serving: 132; Carbohydrates:1.3 g; Protein: 4.3g; Fat: 12.2g

Traditional Doughnuts Keto-Approved

Serves: 4
Cooking Time: 20 minutes

Ingredients:

- ¾ cup almond flour
- ¼ cup flaxseed meal
- ¼ cup erythritol
- 1 teaspoon vanilla extract
- 2 large eggs, beaten
- 3 tablespoons coconut oil
- ¼ cup coconut milk
- 1 tablespoon cocoa powder

Directions:

6. Place all ingredients in a mixing bowl.
7. Mix until well-combined.
8. Scoop the dough into individual doughnut molds.
9. Preheat the air fryer for 5 minutes.
10. Cook for 20 minutes at 350OF.
11. Bake in batches if possible.

Nutrition Information:
Calories per serving: 222; Carbohydrates: 5.1g; Protein: 3.9g; Fat: 20.7g

Crunchy Toffee Topped Cracker Bites

Serves: 15
Cooking Time: 55 minutes

Ingredients:

- 2 cups almond flour
- 1 large egg
- 2 tbsp salted butter melted
- 1/2 tsp salt
- 1/2 tsp baking powder

Topping Ingredients:

- Pinch salt
- 2 tbsp powdered Swerve Sweetener
- 4 ounces Lily's Dark Chocolate chopped
- 2 tsp coconut oil or avocado oil
- 1/2 cup butter
- 1/2 tsp vanilla extract
- 3/4 cup Swerve Sweetener
- 3/4 cup chopped toasted pecans

Directions:

1. Preheat oven to 300oF.
2. Whisk well baking powder, salt, and almond flour in a large bowl. Stir in melted butter and egg until the dough comes together.
3. Turn the dough out onto a large piece of parchment paper and pat into a rough rectangle. Top with another piece of parchment paper and roll into 1/8-inch thick dough, as evenly as you can. Remove the top piece of parchment paper.

4. Using a sharp knife, score the dough into 2-inch squares. Transfer the parchment to a large cookie sheet and bake until the edges are golden brown, and the crackers are firm to the touch, around 35 to 40 minutes.

5. Remove from oven and cool completely.

6. To make the toffee preheat oven to 375oF. Line a baking sheet, about 11x17 inches, with foil and spray lightly with coconut oil spray.

7. Break cracker Arrange the crackers in a single layer so that they are touching, covering as much of the sheet as you can.

8. On medium fire, place a medium saucepan, mix Swerve and butter. Whisk until Swerve is dissolved. Bring to a boil and cook without stirring until mixture darkens to an amber hue, about 5 to 7 minutes.

9. Remove from heat and stir in vanilla extract and salt. If the mixture appears to be separating, stir in 2 tbsp of powdered Swerve Sweetener until it comes back together.

10. Pour the hot toffee immediately over the crackers as evenly as possible to cover. Bake for 5 to 6 minutes, until bubbly. Let cool.

11. Meanwhile, combine the oil and chopped chocolate in a microwave safe bowl and melt on high in 30 second increments, stirring in between. Alternatively, you can melt them together double boiler style.

12. Drizzle the chocolate over the cooled toffee and spread evenly. Sprinkle immediately with the chopped pecans. Let set until the chocolate is firm.

13. Break into pieces. Serve and enjoy or store.

Nutrition Information:

Calories per serving: 120; Carbohydrates: 3.5g; Protein: 2.3g; Fat: 10.7g

Copycat Keto-Approved Almond Joy

Serves: 16
Cooking Time: 8 minutes

Ingredients:

- 6 Tbsp organic cocoa
- 4 Tbsp organic erythritol
- 1 tsp vanilla
- 1/2 cup organic coconut oil
- 1/2 cup organic almond butter
- 1/4 cup xylitol

Coconut Topping Ingredients;

- 1 1/2 tsp vanilla
- 1 2/3 cup organic unsweetened coconut flakes
- 1/3 cup xylitol
- 1/4 tsp additional flavoring (optional)
- 2 tsp organic arrowroot powder
- 7 Tbsp coconut oil
- Almond halves or slices (optional)

Directions:

1. On low heat, melt almond butter and coconut oil.
2. Stir in cocoa and erythritol. Mix well.
3. Except for vanilla, mix in remaining ingredients. Stir continuously until slightly thickened, then remove from heat.
4. Stir in the vanilla.

5. Pour the mixture into an 8×8 pan and place in freezer to harden while you make the topping.
6. To make the topping, melt oil in small pan and add coconut flakes. Stir.
7. Mix in remaining ingredients. Simmer and stir until it thickens a bit.
8. Once the chocolate is hardened, gently smooth the coconut mixture on top.
9. Place slivered or whole almonds on top (optional). Place bars back in the freezer until hardened.
10. Slice into squares of desired size and enjoy!

Nutrition Information:
Calories per serving: 220; Carbohydrates: 7.9g; Protein: 2.3g; Fat: 19.9g

Sea Salt 'n Macadamia Choco Barks

Serves: 10
Cooking Time: 5 minutes
Ingredients:

- 1 teaspoon sea salt flakes
- 1/4 cup (32 g) macadamia nuts, crushed
- 2 Tablespoons (24 g) erythritol or stevia, to taste
- 2 Tablespoons (30 ml) coconut oil, melted
- 3.5 oz (100 g) 100% dark chocolate, broken into pieces

Directions:

1. Melt the chocolate and coconut oil over a very low heat.
2. Remove from heat. Stir in sweetener.
3. Pour the mixture into a loaf pan and place in the fridge for 15 minutes.
4. Scatter the crushed macadamia nuts on top along with the sea salt. Lightly press into the chocolate.
5. Place back into the fridge or freezer for 2 hours.

Nutrition Information:
Calories per serving: 84; Carbohydrates: 1g; Protein: 2g; Fat: 8g

Keto-Approved Lemon Gummies

Serves: 4
Cooking Time: 15 minutes
Ingredients:

- 1/4 cup (60 ml) fresh lemon juice
- 1 Tablespoon (15 ml) water
- 2 Tablespoons (12 g) gelatin powder
- 2 Tablespoons (24 g) erythritol or stevia, to taste

Directions:

1. In a small saucepan, heat up water and lemon juice.
2. Slowly stir in the gelatin powder and erythritol. Heating and mixing well until dissolved.

3. Pour into silicone molds.
4. Freeze or refrigerate for 2+ hours until firm.

Nutrition Information:
Calories per serving: 16; Carbohydrates: 1g; Protein: 3g; Fat: 0g

Keto White Choco Fatty Fudge

Serves: 6
Cooking Time: 10 minutes

Ingredients:

- 1/4 cup coconut butter
- 1/4 cup cashew butter
- 2 tbsp coconut oil
- 2 tbsp cacao butter
- 1/4 teaspoon vanilla powder
- 10–12 drops liquid stevia, or to taste

Directions:

1. Over low heat place a small saucepan and melt coconut oil, cacao butter, cashew butter, and coconut butter.
2. Remove from the heat and stir in the vanilla and stevia.
3. Pour into a silicone mold and place in the freezer for 30 minutes.
4. Store in the fridge for a softer consistency.

Nutrition Information:
Calories per serving: 221; Carbohydrates: 1.7g; Protein: 0.2g; Fat: 23.7g

Keto Approved Mouth-Watering Truffles

Serves: 10
Cooking Time: 5 minutes

Ingredients:

- 1 cup coconut cream
- extra cocoa powder for dusting
- 1/4 teaspoon espresso powder optional
- 1/4 teaspoon kosher salt
- 1/4 teaspoon xanthan gum
- 2-4 tablespoons xylitol or allulose, to taste
- 2-4 tablespoons cocoa powder use the smaller amount for milk chocolate and the larger for dark

Directions:

1. On medium fire, place espresso powder, cocoa, sweetened, and coconut cream on a saucepan.
2. Once melted, puree with an immersion blender until fully blended.
3. Sprinkle xanthan gum little by little and blend until fully combined. If the mixture is too thick to mix, add 1 teaspoon of water at a time being mindful that you want it thick for the truffles to hold their shape.
4. Remove from heat, allow the mixture to cool completely, cover and refrigerate until set.
5. Scoop chocolate to form 1-inch rounds. Dust your palms with cocoa powder and roll until smooth. Work quickly to avoid melting them, and if they become too soft just pop in the freezer for 10 minutes before continuing.
6. Serve and enjoy.

Nutrition Information:
Calories per serving: 84; Carbohydrates: 2.1g; Protein: 1g; Fat: 8g

Eggnog Keto Custard

Serves: 8
Cook Time: 10 minutes
Ingredients:

- ¼ tsp nutmeg
- ¼ Truvia
- ½ cup heavy whipping cream
- 1 cup half and half
- 4 eggs

Directions:

1. Blend all ingredients together
2. Pour evenly into 6 ramekins (microwave safe)
3. Microwave at 50% power for 4 minutes then stir thoroughly
4. Microwave for another 3-4 minutes at 50% power then stir well again
5. Serve either cool or hot

Nutrition Information:
Calories per serving: 70; Carbs: 1g; Fats: 6g; Protein: 3g

Keto Dark-Choco Cream Cheese Candy

Serves: 16
Cooking Time: 10 minutes

Ingredients:

- 1 cup butter
- 1 cup low carb powdered sweetener Sukrin Melis
- 1 cup unsweetened almond butter or peanut butter
- 1 teaspoon stevia concentrated powder see note
- 1 teaspoon vanilla extract
- 1/3 cup unsweetened cocoa powder
- 1-ounce unsweetened baking chocolate can add 2 ounces to up flavor
- 8 ounces cream cheese

Directions:

1. Line an 8x8 baking pan with parchment paper.
2. Melt together butter and baking chocolate over medium heat.
3. Add almond butter and blend in with an electric mixer.
4. Mix in the cream cheese.
5. Remove from heat and stir in remaining dry ingredients.
6. Blend thoroughly. Whisk in vanilla extract
7. Spread mixture into prepared pan evenly. Chill in refrigerator until set.
8. Evenly cut into 16-squares and enjoy.

Nutrition Information:

Calories per serving: 270; Carbohydrates: 5g; Protein: 4g; Fat: 26g

Chapter 10 Custard, Cheesecakes and Mousse

Avocado-Based Choco Mousse

Serves: 4
Cooking Time: 0 minutes
Ingredients:

- 1 teaspoon pure vanilla extract
- 1/4 cup Almond Breeze Unsweetened Almond Milk-Cashew milk Blend
- 1/8 teaspoon kosher salt
- 2 large, ripe avocados
- 3 tablespoons unsweetened cocoa powder
- 4 ounces chopped semisweet chocolate

Directions:

1. In microwave safe bowl, place Choco chips and microwave in 15-second interval while mixing every after microwaving until melted.
2. In food processor, add melted chocolate and remaining ingredients and puree until smooth and creamy.
3. Evenly divide into glasses and refrigerate for two hours before serving.

Nutrition Information:
Calories per serving: 383; Protein: 6.0g; Carbs: 29.0g; Fat: 27.0g

Orange and Chocolate Mousse

Serves: 4
Cook Time: 40 minutes
Ingredients:

- Pinch of salt
- 2 tbsp cacao powder
- ¼ cup sweetener
- 1 orange
- 1 tsp vanilla
- 2 large eggs
- 1 cup heavy whipping cream
- 1 cup unsweetened macadamia milk

Directions:

1. Preheat oven to 325 degrees F and star boiling the kettle
2. Blend all the ingredients together and evenly distribute to four ramekins
3. Put ramekins on top of a baking dish and pour boiling water into the dish
4. Bake in the oven for 30-40 minutes
5. Remove from water and let cool

Nutrition Information:
Calories per serving: 75; Carbs: 4g; Fats: 1g; Protein:5g

Sugar Free Chocolate Custard

Serves: 4
Cook Time: 30 minutes
Ingredients:

- 1 orange
- ¾ tsp stevia
- 2 tbsp dark cocoa
- 2 tbsp erythritol
- 250 milliliters heavy cream
- 2 eggs

Directions:

1. Preheat oven to 160 degrees C
2. Bring orange zest and cream to below boiling point then take off heat
3. Blend rest of ingredients together with cream mixture
4. Pour mix evenly to 4 ramekins and bake for 20 minutes
5. Then let cool and refrigerate for 4 hours

Nutrition Information:
Calories per serving: 343; Carbs: 2g; Fats: 35g; Protein: 5g

Maple Bacon Custard

Serves: 2
Cook Time: 30 minutes

Ingredients:

- 3 slices of bacon (optional for garnish)
- 1 tsp cinnamon
- ½ tsp maple extract
- 40 drops liquid stevia
- 1 ½ tsp bacon grease
- 2 large egg yolks
- 1 cup heavy whipping cream

Directions:

1. Preheat oven to 300 degrees F
2. Cook three slices of bacon and keep the grease
3. Mix rest of ingredients together and then mix in cooled bacon grease
4. Place 2 ramekins on a casserole dish
5. Evenly put batter into the 2 ramekins
6. Put boiling water in the casserole dish
7. Bake in oven for 30 minutes
8. Cool in fridge for 2 hours and garnish with bacon if wanted

Nutrition Information:
Calories per serving: 464; Carbs: 5g; Fats: 48g; Protein: 3g

Keto Lemon Custard

Serves: 8
Cook Time: 50 minutes

Ingredients:

- 1 Lemon
- 6 large eggs
- 2 tbsp lemon zest
- 1 cup Lakanto
- 2 cups heavy cream

Directions:

1. Preheat oven to 300 degrees F
2. Mix all ingredients together
3. Pour mixture into ramekins
4. Put ramekins into a dish with boiling water
5. Bake in oven for 45-50 minutes
6. Let cool then refrigerate for 2 hours
7. Use lemon slices as garnish

Nutritional Information:

Calories per serving: 233; Carbs: 4g; Fats: 21g; Protein: 7g

No Bake Lemon Cheese-Stard

Serves: 8
Cooking Time: 0 minutes

Ingredients:

- 1 tsp vanilla flavoring
- 1 tbsp lemon juice
- 1 tsp liquid low carb sweetener (Splenda)
- 1 tsp stevia glycerite
- 2 oz heavy cream
- 8 oz softened cream cheese

Directions:

1. Mix all ingredients in a large mixing bowl until the mixture has a pudding consistency.
2. Pour the mixture to small serving cups and refrigerate for a few hours until it sets.
3. Serve chilled.

Nutritional Information:
Calories per serving: 111; Carbs: 1.4g; Fats: 10.7g; Protein: 2.2g

Made in the USA
Lexington, KY
27 June 2019